universe publishing

contents

in action

chewing

Teething puppies will gnaw on sneakers and slippers. For saliva-free shoes provide a chew toy or two.

chewing

chewing

chewing

chewing

chewing

listening

Puppies turn heads—and
not only for the obvious
reasons. They cock their heads
in the direction of noise.

listening.

listening

listening

listening

listening

listening

cuddling

A sense of security comes from close contact, which is why puppies prefer resting against a companion or two—or three.

cuddling

cuddling

cuddling

cuddling

cuddling

cuddling

cuddling

licking

Stress relief is just a lick of the nose away for puppies. If only it were so easy for their human companions . . .

 licking

licking

licking

licking

licking

licking

licking

licking

licking

licking

licking

licking

begging

When puppies extend their heads up toward friendly hands the effort is rewarded with soothing strokes.

begging

begging

begging

begging

begging

begging

romping

Romping around is a way for puppies to let off steam and to bond with their canine and human friends.

romping

romping

romping

rolling

Relaxed, happy puppies
make it known when tummy
rubs are welcome.

rolling

rolling

rolling

rolling

rolling

rolling

rolling

gh-fiving

Raising their paws is a way for puppies to say, "I know you're the boss (or I'll *pretend* you're the boss) . . . now please pat my head."

high-fiving

high-fiving

high-fiving

high-fiving

high-fiving

high-fiving

high-fiving

sleeping

Puppies live a life of leisure,
spending their days getting
as much sleep as they need
(which is a lot).

sleeping.

sleeping

sleeping

sleeping

sleeping.

sleeping

sleeping

stretching

Some puppies like to extend
themselves completely when
they take a play break.

stretching

stretching

stretching

panting

Are puppies hot or tense, or are they sharing their enthusiasm about an upcoming walk? Panting has multiple purposes.

panting

panting

panting

panting

scratching

Everyone has to scratch an itch once in a while and puppies are no exception.

scratching

scratching

wagging

Puppies express many feelings—from happiness to aggressiveness and fear—with the help of their telling tails.

wagging

wagging

wagging

watching

Eyes reveal a range of puppy moods, from fear to boredom, shyness to playfulness.

watching

watching

watching

watching

watching

135

nuzzling

Puppies rub noses for the same reasons humans shake hands—it's a way to greet new companions.

nuzzling

relaxing

Puppies need their downtime,
but with their heads up they
might be ready for fun, too.

relaxing

relaxing

relaxing

relaxing

relaxing

relaxing

speaking

"I'm angry," "I'm bored," "I want to scare you," and even "C'mon, let's play!" are what different puppy barks can say.

speaking

speaking

speaking

speaking

speaking

waiting

Patience is a virtue, as obedient puppies who sit and wait know. Restraint often is rewarded with tasty treats.

waiting

waiting

waiting

waiting

waiting

waiting

yawning

Puppies relieve tense situations—standoffs with other puppies or their own nervousness—with full-muzzle yawns.

Yawning

yawning

yawning

yawning

Yawning

yawning

yawning

yawning

sniffing

Smell first, then advance.
Puppies' sensitive snouts
tell them a lot about
potential playmates.

sniffing

183

resting

Is it naptime? Sleepy puppies need to catch some z's before springing into action again.

resting

resting

resting

resting

190

resting

resting

resting

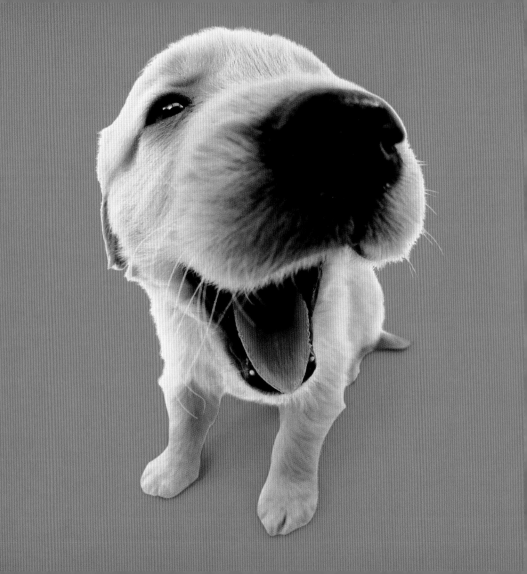

laughing

Puppies like to show off their pearly whites when they feel happy, not only when they want to be scary.

laughing

laughing

laughing

laughing

laughing.

laughing

grinning

Polite puppies approach
new human friends with
smiles to show they are
eager for a meet and greet.

grinning

ologizing

Puppies know when "I'm sorry" is in order. Luckily for them, looking remorseful works wonders.

apologizing

apologizing

apologizing

211

apologizing

posing

Postures that say "I'm content,"
"I'm relaxed," "I'm obedient,"
or "I want to play!" are all part
of the puppy repertoire.

posing

posing

posing

219

posing

First published in the United States of America in 2005
by **UNIVERSE PUBLISHING**
A Division of Rizzoli International Publications, Inc.
300 Park Avenue South
New York, NY 10010
www.rizzoliusa.com

© 2005 artlist INTERNATIONAL

Text by: Tricia Levi
Design by: Susi Oberhelman

2005 2006 2007 2008 2009 / 10 9 8 7 6 5 4 3 2 1

Printed in the United States

ISBN: 0-7893-1315-4

Library of Congress Catalog Control Number: 2005902613